MAURICE RAVEL

LE TOMBEAU DE COUPERIN

Solo Piano

Edited by / Herausgegeben von / Édition de
Roger Nichols

Urtext

EIGENTUM DES VERLEGERS · ALLE RECHTE VORBEHALTEN
ALL RIGHTS RESERVED

EDITION PETERS

LONDON · FRANKFURT/M. · LEIPZIG · NEW YORK

CONTENTS

Ravel's Piano Music - A New Edition

page

Preface 4
Préface 6
Vorwort 9

Le tombeau de Couperin

I: Prélude 12
II: Fugue 17
III: Forlane 20
IV: Rigaudon 26
V: Menuet 30
VI: Toccata 34

Critical Commentary 43

RAVEL'S PIANO MUSIC - A NEW EDITION

Editorial Method and Sources

There is no denying the excitement of holding in one's hand the autograph manuscript of a musical masterpiece; and where the autograph is itself a work of art, as many of Ravel's are, then aesthetic considerations also come into play to compound the excitement. But there is equally no denying that composers are, like all mortals, fallible, and that however beautiful and exciting an autograph is, it may nonetheless contain mistakes. The apparently laudable desire to go back to what the composer originally wrote needs therefore to be tempered with a certain amount of common sense.

With stage works, it is true, pressures of time, space, money and personalities often lead to deformations which the composer does not in any sense welcome but has to accept if the performance is to go ahead, and which may then find their way into the printed score. But in the case of piano works, the pressures on the composer in preparing an edition are much slighter, exerted for the most part by the printer in his desire for conformity with house style, so that changes introduced between manuscript and edition have a somewhat greater chance of representing decisions freely taken by the composer. Certainly, in the process of publication mistakes may be introduced as well as rectified and, when musicality and common sense indicate that this may have happened, the autograph can indeed sometimes provide vital evidence. But in the course of conversations with a number of composers of our own time, I am given overwhelmingly to understand that they would actually be angry if future editors ignored their carefully prepared printed scores and went back automatically to their original autographs for a so-called true reading.

In the case of Ravel's piano music, such a critical view of autograph evidence is more than ever justified, since the Music Department of the Bibliothèque Nationale holds a bound volume containing Ravel's own printed copies, with autograph corrections, of the bulk of the first editions of his solo piano music.[1] To judge from the contents, the volume would appear to have been made up between 1911 and 1913. The works missing from this collection are *Sérénade grotesque*, *Sites auriculaires*, *Ma Mère l'Oye*, *Prélude*, *A la manière de...*, *Le tombeau de Couperin* and *Frontispice*. Printed copies with autograph corrections of *Ma Mère l'Oye* and *A la manière de...* are held separately in the same institution,[2] while Ravel's own printed copy of *Le tombeau de Couperin*, with autograph fingerings and one autograph correction, is on display in the Musée Ravel at Montfort l'Amaury. For *Sérénade grotesque* and *Sites auriculaires* the autographs may be said to assume paramount importance since these pieces were not published in the composer's lifetime. The autograph of *Frontispice* is also significant because Ravel's own printed copy has not been found. Unfortunately, for *Prélude* neither the autograph nor the composer's printed copy is extant.

No proofs are known to survive of the first editions of any of Ravel's piano works, apart from a set of first proofs of *Le tombeau de Couperin* in the Durand archives, marked up by the Durand editor with a request for second proofs (I am grateful to Roy Howat for providing me with a copy of this material). This set contains no autograph markings. All the editorial annotations found their way into the first edition except for the form of some of the multiple appoggiaturas in 'Prélude' and 'Forlane', over which Ravel would seem to have changed his mind.

Primary Sources

Where Ravel's own corrected edition is available, I have taken it as my main primary source; discrepancies between this corrected edition (**CE**), the first printed edition (**E**) and the autograph (**A**) are duly noted. A further primary source is the set of printed editions belonging to Vlado Perlemuter, who studied almost all Ravel's piano works with the composer in 1927 (**PerCE**). These copies carry some valuable additions and corrections in Ravel's own hand, mainly for *Gaspard de la nuit*. They also carry additions and corrections dictated by Ravel, but in Perlemuter's hand; these have not been treated as primary evidence. The copies belonging to Robert Casadesus are now in the possession of his widow, but Mme Casadesus has been kind enough to assure me that they contain no markings in the composer's hand. Likewise, Jacques Février's niece and pupil Mme Aboulker-Rosenfeld has assured me that her uncle's copies contain no markings beyond his fingerings.

Secondary Sources

The secondary sources fall into four groups:

(a) Printed copies with corrections by Lucien Garban (**GarCE**). Garban worked for the Durand publishing house and was a close friend of the composer. The exact status of these corrections is impossible to determine but, given the links between the two men, it is feasible that at least some of the changes were dictated by Ravel. These copies are now in the library of Bakersfield College, California. Garban also made piano duet transcriptions of *Valses nobles et sentimentales* and *Le tombeau de Couperin* (**GarT**). These are published by Durand.

(b) Ravel's own orchestrations of a number of his piano pieces (**RO**). In chronological order of original composition (dates of orchestration in brackets), these are: *Menuet antique* (1929), 'Habanera' from *Sites auriculaires* (1908), *Pavane pour une Infante défunte* (1910), 'Une barque sur l'océan' and 'Alborada del gracioso' from *Miroirs* (1906 and 1923), *Ma Mère l'Oye* (1911), *Valses nobles et sentimentales* (1912), 'Prélude', 'Forlane', 'Menuet' and 'Rigaudon' from *Le tombeau de Couperin* (1919).

(c) Recordings

(i) Piano rolls made by Ravel (**RR**) in 1913 for Welte-Mignon (*Sonatine*, movements I and II, C2887; *Valses nobles et sentimentales*, C2888), and in 1922 for Duo-Art (*Pavane pour une Infante défunte*, 084; 'Oiseaux tristes' from *Miroirs*, 082). It was claimed that at this second session Ravel also recorded 'Le gibet' from *Gaspard de la nuit* and the 'Toccata' from *Le tombeau de Couperin*, but these were in fact recorded by Robert Casadesus. It remains uncertain which of the two recorded 'La vallée des cloches' from *Miroirs* in 1929 for Duo-Art (72750), though I am almost certain it was Ravel. All these recordings have been transferred a number of times to LP, but unfortunately the piano roll equipment has not always been properly regulated.

(ii) Recordings made on disc by three pianists, all of whom had the benefit of the composer's detailed advice: Robert Casadesus (1955, CBS 13062–4[3]); Jacques Février (1972, ADES 7041–4); Vlado Perlemuter (1961, VOX VBX 410 1–3[4]; 1977, NIMBUS 2101–3, reissued CD NI 5005, 5011) (**CasR, FévR, PerRI and PerRII**). Marcelle Meyer, although known to Ravel (together they gave the private two-piano performance of *La valse* which failed to impress Diaghilev), never studied his piano music with him, as her daughter, Marie Bertin, was good enough to inform me. I have therefore taken no account of Mme Meyer's Ravel recordings reissued by EMI on the Référence label.

(d) Souvenirs of Ravel as a coach of his piano music

(i) from Vlado Perlemuter in his interviews with Hélène Jourdan-Morhange, published as *Ravel d'après Ravel* (Lausanne, 1953) and in an English translation by F. Tanner as *Ravel according to Ravel* (New York/London, 1988; 2/1991) (**PerS(HJM)**).

(ii) from Vlado Perlemuter in conversation with the Editor of the present edition (**PerS(conv)**).

(iii) from Henriette Faure in *Mon maître Maurice Ravel* (Paris, 1978) (**FauS**). Mlle Faure, the sister of the politician Edgar Faure, was coached by Ravel for her recital of his music – in all probability the first ever all-Ravel piano recital – which she gave at the Théâtre des Champs-Elysées on 12 January 1923 (not 18 January, as she states in her book), when she was eighteen. Other souvenirs are fully identified *in situ*.

The secondary sources are considered when they shed further light on an established text, or when problems in the text are not fully elucidated by the primary sources.

Acknowledgements

I should like to express my gratitude to the following for their assistance: to Gaby Casadesus for information about her husband Robert; to Dr Michel Noiray, who told me about the autograph of *Sonatine* and helped me to obtain a copy; to James Segesta, reference librarian of California State College, Bakersfield, for sending me copies of Lucien Garban's corrected scores; to Jean Touzelet for allowing me to hear Ravel's Duo-Art piano rolls on a machine in superb order; and to Dr J. Rigbie Turner, Curator of Music Manuscripts and Books in the Pierpont Morgan Library, New York, for sending me copies of the autographs of *Jeux d'eau*, and of 'Noctuelles' and 'Oiseaux tristes' from *Miroirs*. I am grateful also to two performers: to Roy Howat for advice that has blended the scholarly with the practical; and to Vlado Perlemuter for talking to me about his lessons with Ravel and for allowing me to study his copies of the music. Finially, my thanks go to the staff of the Music Department of the Bibliothèque Nationale de France, and to Margaret Cobb, Gwendolyn Mok, Jean-Michel Nectoux, Dr Arbie Orenstein, and Dr Stephen Roe for numerous kindnesses; and especially to Graham Hayter of Peters Edition Ltd., London, who has been the mainstay of this Ravel enterprise since its inception, and whose keen eye and musical expertise have made him (as Debussy said of André Caplet) 'the graveyard of errors'.

Roger Nichols
1991

Table of Source abbreviations

A: autograph

E: first edition

CE: Ravel's corrected copy of the first edition

PerCE: Perlemuter's printed copy with Ravel's additions and corrections

GarCE: printed copies with Garban's additions and corrections

GarT: Garban's piano duet transcriptions

RO: Ravel's orchestral transcriptions

RR: Ravel's recordings on piano roll

CasR: recordings by Casadesus

FévR: recordings by Février

PerRI and **PerRII**: recordings by Perlemuter[5]

PerS(HJM): souvenirs from Perlemuter in *Ravel d'après Ravel*, in conversation with Hélène Jourdan-Morhange[6]

PerS(conv): souvenirs from Perlemuter in conversation with the present Editor

FauS: souvenirs from Faure in *Mon maître Maurice Ravel*

[1] Vma. 2967
[2] Vma. 3157(7) and Fol. Vm12. 2701(2)A respectively
[3] Reissued SONY MH2K 63316
[4] Reissued VOX CDX2 5507
[5] The designation **PerR** without a number indicates that Perlemuter's two recordings coincide over the point in question
[6] Dual page numbers refer to the French and English editions respectively

LE TOMBEAU DE COUPERIN

Preface

Writing to his friend Roland-Manuel on 1 October 1914, Ravel informed him that he had "begun 2 series of piano pieces: 1. a French suite – no, it isn't what you think: *La Marseillaise* won't be in it, but it'll have a forlane and a gigue; no tango, though; 2. a *Romantic Night*, with spleen, infernal hunt, accursed nun etc.".[1] The tango reference was to the ban recently placed on this dance by the Archbishop of Paris as being lascivious and offensive to public morals (see also below). It may well be that Ravel was more serious about the gigue and the *Romantic Night*, but in the event the forlane was the only item to survive.

Ravel had begun the suite in July of that year, but we have only patchy evidence as to how much of it was written before he enlisted as an army truck driver in March 1915. Marcel Marnat says that the title *Le tombeau de Couperin* was chosen before the war and thus should not be seen as having initially had any funereal intent;[2] and indeed the composer himself said that "the tribute is directed not so much to the individual figure of Couperin as to the whole of French music of the eighteenth century".[3] But it is absolutely clear, both from Ravel's ultimate dedication of the six pieces to friends killed in action and from the funerary urn he himself designed for the inner cover of the first edition, that when he returned to it on his temporary discharge from the army in June 1917, it had acquired strong memorial associations. We may even extend these to include his mother, whose death in January 1917 left him desolate and from which many of his friends thought he never really recovered, as well as the whole Western European civilisation that he felt had reached its apogee in his beloved eighteenth century and was now gone forever.

On 7 July 1917, Ravel wrote to his publisher Jacques Durand, "The *Tombeau de Couperin* is coming on. The menuet and rigaudon are done. The rest is taking shape".[4] From this we may deduce that the extant sketches for the 'Musette' of the 'Menuet' and for the 'Prélude' and 'Forlane'[5] date from this time. Thereafter nothing is known of the suite's progress until Marguerite Long gave the first performance at the Salle Gaveau on 11 April 1919, although rumour had it that Ravel did not want this performance to take place until the war was over. The work was a great success and had to be encored in its entirety.[6] Marnat points rightly to the influence of Rameau and Scarlatti in the keyboard writing (both composers were possibly more popular in France then than they are now) and quotes with approval Antoine Goléa's judgment that the work represents "the courageous, clear-eyed synthesis of almost one hundred and fifty years of music, from [Mozart's] *Bastien et Bastienne* to [Albéniz's] *Iberia*".[7]

According to Marguerite Long, Ravel's chief requirement in the 'Prélude' was that he should be able to hear all the notes.[8] This was no doubt true as regards the notes in ordinary type, but for the ornaments, both here and elsewhere in the work, Ravel was insistent not only that they should be played on the beat, but that the strongest accent should be on the initial note of the ornament with a diminuendo, even a blurring, on the notes that follow. He also wanted a little air ("*respirations*") between the phrases.[9]

For the 'Fugue', he asked for the use just of the fingers, with no movement of the wrist;[10] and the very detailed fingering in his own copy, reproduced in the present edition, suggests that he also used very little if any pedal.

As mentioned above, the 'Forlane' seems to have been the earliest movement Ravel decided on. In a letter that is undated but which certainly comes from the summer of 1914, he wrote from the Basque country to his friend Cipa Godebski:

> "…I'm slogging away on behalf of the Pope. You know that this august personage has just launched a new dance, the Forlane. I'm transcribing one by Couperin. I'm going to arrange for it to be danced at the Vatican by Mistinguet and Colette in drag. Don't be surprised by this return to religion. It's being in my native surroundings that does it."[11]

The forlane, originally a gondoliers' dance, was the only dance permitted to be performed in front of the Pontiff owing to its formal, non-erotic nature. Polite Parisian society tried to substitute it for the treacherous tango when the latter was banned, but without success.[12]

The forlane Ravel transcribed was the last of the seven movements of François Couperin's fourth *Concert royal*.[13] He kept Couperin's structure of *rondeaux* interspersed with three *couplets* (ABACADA), though the final return of the *rondeau*, limited to the last six and a half bars, is no more than an echo of its original statement; and whereas Couperin's 'Forlane' is in E major with the third *couplet* in the minor, Ravel reverses the modes and extends this final *couplet* with some of the most extraordinary harmonies even he ever invented (bars 140–156). Most of these bars contain nine or ten notes of the chromatic scale and bars 149 and 150 each contain all twelve. It is not really surprising that when Marguerite Long played this passage to the conductor Camille Chevillard (born 1859), he put his hands over his ears.[14]

The 'Rigaudon' and the 'Menuet' were the two movements of the suite that Ravel was happy to play in public, notably on his American tour in 1928. In the former, he asked Henriette Faure again to take care over the "*respirations*" and to be implacable in tempo.[15] The 'Menuet', his fourth and last published essay in this form after the *Menuet antique* (1895), the central movement of the *Sonatine* (1903–5) and the *Menuet sur le nom d'Haydn* (1909), is perhaps more complex than it seems at first sight. As in the first two examples above, Ravel juxtaposes two ideas at the reprise – here the 'Musette' continues under the return of the opening tune – but this double perspective can be traced on another level to a much earlier point in the piece, namely bars 9–24 where, as Françoise Gervais has pointed out, Ravel's phrasing is at odds with the natural inflections of the melody.[16] We may also note that in the first eight bars the right-hand articulation is organised palindromically – stressed/legato/legato/stressed – while the left hand cuts across this with phrasing of its own. (As a further complication, in Ravel's orchestral version the left-hand phrasing is essentially the same as in the piano original, but the oboe's phrasing of the tune is quite different).

The suite is crowned by the 'Toccata', the end of which Ravel claimed was pure Saint-Saëns[17] – in his mouth, a compliment to the excellence of its workmanship. The climax, according to Henri Gil-Marchex, "requires an independence of arm which has to be acquired specially, even after one has studied Liszt's *Transcendental Studies*",[18] and Perlemuter concurs that it is a virtuoso piece and has to be played as such.[19]

Of the dedicatees, Jacques Charlot was a cousin of Ravel's publisher Jacques Durand and worked for the family firm – he was also the dedicatee of the second movement of Debussy's *En blanc et noir*; Jean Cruppi, who finally replaced Sergeant Baguerion-Desormeaux as the dedicatee of the 'Fugue', was the son of Mme Jean Cruppi whose influence had been crucial in persuading the Opéra-Comique to mount Ravel's *L'heure espagnole* in 1911; Gabriel Deluc was an old friend from Saint-Jean-de-Luz; Pierre and Pascal Gaudin were twins whom Ravel had known as children – they were killed by the same shell on the day they arrived at the front; Jean Dreyfus was Roland-Manuel's half-brother; and Joseph, Marquis de Marliave was a professional soldier with a deep interest in music who married Marguerite Long in 1906.

Editorial Practice

Square brackets have been applied to the majority of editorial additions: metronome markings, accidentals, rests, dynamics, articulation, *main droite/main gauche* indications, fingering (where completion of Ravel's minimal indications for chords is necessary), *subito*, *simile* and *loco* markings, and pedal indications. Precautionary accidentals from E, with or without round brackets, have, where considered helpful, been retained. The fingerings are all taken from Ravel's corrected copy of the first edition (CE), with the exception of the indication at bar 87 of 'Prélude' (right-hand thumb) which is printed in E.

The pedal indications are those of E. The editorial pedalling concerning the application or release of "1 Corde" is supported by notes in the Critical Commentary.

Phrase marks and slurs have been added or amended so as to conform with parallel passages. These changes, together with any additional *laisser vibrer* ties and staccato dots, are not distinguished in the music text, but are detailed in the Critical Commentary. All irrational rhythmic groupings are here indicated as such.

Roger Nichols
1995

[1] M. Ravel: *Lettres, écrits, entretiens*, ed. A. Orenstein, (Paris, 1989; Eng. trans. A. Orenstein, New York, 1990), 155–6

[2] M. Marnat: *Maurice Ravel*, (Paris, 1986), 437

[3] 'Esquisse autobiographique', *La Revue Musicale*, (Dec 1938), 22

[4] *Ravel au miroir de ses lettres*, ed. M. Gerar and R. Chalupt, (Paris, 1956), 150

[5] A. Orenstein: *Ravel, man and musician*, (New York, 1975), 211–12

[6] *see* (1), 185

[7] *see* (2), 436–7; quotation from A. Goléa: *Esthétique de la musique contemporaine*, (Paris, 1954)

[8] M. Long: *Au piano avec Ravel*, (Paris, 1971; Eng. trans. O. Senior-Ellis, London, 1973), 94

[9] FauS 88

[10] *ibid.*

[11] *see* (4), 106

[12] *ibid.*; *see also* (2), 387

[13] A. Orenstein: 'Some unpublished music and letters by Maurice Ravel', *Music Forum*, iii (1973), 330–31 (plates xiii a and b)

[14] *see* (8), 96

[15] *see* (9)

[16] F. Gervais: 'Ambiguités raveliennes', *Maurice Ravel au XXe siècle*, (Paris, 1976), 21

[17] H. Jourdan-Morhange in PerS(HJM) 75/79

[18] H. Gil-Marchex: 'La technique de piano', *La Revue Musicale*, (April 1925), 44

[19] PerS(HJM) 74/78

LA MUSIQUE POUR PIANO DE RAVEL – UNE NOUVELLE ÉDITION
Principes d'édition et sources

Nul ne niera combien il est émouvant de tenir en main le manuscrit autographe d'un chef-d'œuvre musical ; et lorsque l'autographe est lui-même une œuvre d'art, comme c'est souvent le cas de ceux de Ravel, cette émotion est encore renforcée par les considérations esthétiques. Mais nul ne niera non plus que les compositeurs sont, comme tous les mortels, faillibles, et qu'un autographe, si beau et si émouvant soit-il, peut néanmoins comporter des erreurs. Le désir louable de retourner à ce que le compositeur a écrit à l'origine demande donc à être tempéré par un certain bon sens.

Avec les œuvres scéniques, il est vrai que les questions de temps, de lieu, d'argent et de personnes conduisent souvent à des déformations dont le compositeur ne se réjouit nullement, mais qu'il doit accepter pour que la représentation aille de l'avant, et qui peuvent se trouver incorporées à la partition imprimée. Mais, dans le cas d'œuvres pour piano, les pressions sur le compositeur dans la préparation d'une édition sont bien moindres, exercées pour l'essentiel par l'éditeur, qui souhaite qu'elle se conforme aux usages de la maison, si bien que les changements introduits entre le manuscrit et l'édition ont une plus grande chance de représenter des décisions librement prises par le compositeur. Certes, dans le processus de publication, des erreurs peuvent aussi bien être introduites que rectifiées, et lorsque la musicalité et le bon sens indiquent que c'est le cas, l'autographe peut effectivement apporter un témoignage crucial. Mais des conversations avec un certain nombre de compositeurs de notre temps m'ont convaincu qu'ils seraient en fait très agacés si les futurs éditeurs ignoraient leurs partitions soigneusement préparées et retourneraient automatiquement à leurs autographes originaux pour une lecture prétendument véridique.

Dans le cas de la musique pour piano de Ravel, une telle vision critique des documents autographes est plus que jamais justifiée, puisque le département de la musique de la Bibliothèque nationale de France possède un volume contenant les exemplaires imprimés de Ravel lui-même, avec des corrections autographes, de la plupart des premières éditions de sa musique pour piano seul [1]. À en juger d'après le contenu, le volume semble avoir été réuni entre 1911 et 1913. Les œuvres qui manquent dans cette collection sont : *Sérénade grotesque*, *Sites auriculaires*, *Ma mère l'Oye*, *Prélude*, *À la manière de...*, *Le Tombeau de Couperin* et *Frontispice*. La même bibliothèque conserve séparément des exemplaires imprimés avec corrections autographes de *Ma mère l'Oye* et d'*À la manière de...* [2], tandis que l'exemplaire imprimé personnel de Ravel du *Tombeau de Couperin*, avec doigtés autographes et une correction autographe, est exposé au musée Ravel de Monfort-l'Amaury. Pour la *Sérénade grotesque* et les *Sites auriculaires*, les autographes sont d'une importance capitale, puisque ces œuvres ne furent pas publiées du vivant du compositeur. L'autographe de *Frontispice* est également important, puisque l'on n'a pas retrouvé l'exemplaire imprimé de Ravel. Malheureusement, pour le *Prélude*, ni l'autographe ni l'exemplaire imprimé du compositeur ne nous sont parvenus.

À notre connaissance, il ne subsiste d'épreuves de la première édition d'aucune œuvre pour piano de Ravel, mis à part une série de premières épreuves du *Tombeau de Couperin* dans les archives Durand, marquées par l'éditeur de Durand d'une demande de secondes épreuves (je remercie Roy Howat de m'avoir fourni une copie de ces documents). Ces épreuves ne comportent pas d'indications autographes. Toutes les annotations éditoriales ont été intégrées à la première édition sauf la forme de certaines des appoggiatures multiples dans le « Prélude » et la « Forlane » du *Tombeau de Couperin*, au sujet desquelles Ravel semblerait avoir changé d'avis.

Sources primaires

Lorsque l'édition corrigée de Ravel est disponible, je l'ai prise comme source primaire principale ; les divergences entre cette édition corrigée (**CE**), la première édition imprimée (**E**) et l'autographe sont dûment notées. Une autre source principale est la série d'éditions imprimées ayant appartenu à Vlado Perlemuter, qui étudia presque toutes les œuvres pour piano de Ravel avec le compositeur en 1927 (**PerCE0**). Ces exemplaires contiennent de précieux ajouts et corrections de la main de Ravel, surtout pour *Gaspard de la nuit*. Ils comportent aussi des additions et des corrections dictées par Ravel, mais de la main de Perlemuter ; celles-ci n'ont pas été considérées comme source principale. Les exemplaires de Robert Casadesus sont maintenant en la possession de sa veuve, Mme Casadesus, qui a eu la gentillesse de m'assurer qu'ils ne comportaient pas d'annotations de la main du compositeur. De même, la nièce et élève de Jacques Février, Mme Aboulker-Rosenfeld, m'a confirmé que les exemplaires de son oncle ne contenaient pas d'autres indications que ses doigtés.

Sources secondaires

Les sources secondaires se divisent en quatre groupes :

(a) Quelques exemplaires imprimés avec corrections de Lucien Garban. Garban, qui travaillait pour la maison d'édition Durand, était un ami intime du compositeur. Le statut exact de ces corrections est impossible à déterminer, mais, étant donné les liens entre les deux hommes, il est possible qu'au moins certains des changements aient été dictés par Ravel. Ces exemplaires sont maintenant à la bibliothèque de Bakersfield College, Californie. Garban fit également des transcriptions pour piano à quatre mains des *Valses nobles et sentimentales* et du *Tombeau de Couperin* (**GarT**). Elles sont publiées par Durand.

(b) Les orchestrations faites par Ravel lui-même d'un certain nombre de ses œuvres pour piano (**RO**). Par ordre chronologique des compositions originales (dates d'orchestration entre parenthèses), ce sont : *Menuet antique* (1929), « Habanera » des *Sites auriculaires* (1908), *Pavane pour une infante défunte* (1910), « Une barque sur l'océan » et « Alborada del gracioso » de *Miroirs* (1906 et 1923), *Ma mère l'Oye* (1911), *Valses nobles et sentimentales* (1912), « Prélude », « Forlane », « Menuet » et « Rigaudon » du *Tombeau de Couperin* (1919).

(c) Enregistrements

(i) Rouleaux de piano faits par Ravel en 1913 pour Welte-Mignon (*Sonatine*, mouvements I et II, C2887 ; *Valses nobles et sentimentales*, C2888) et en 1922 pour Duo-Art (*Pavane pour une infante défunte*, 084 ; « Oiseaux tristes » de *Miroirs*, 082). On a dit que lors de cette seconde séance Ravel enregistra également « Le Gibet » de *Gaspard de la nuit* et la « Toccata » du *Tombeau de Couperin*, mais ces pièces furent en fait enregistrées par Robert Casadesus. On ne sait pas avec certitude lequel des deux enregistra « La Vallée des cloches » de *Miroirs* en 1929 pour Duo-Art (72750), encore que je sois presque sûr que c'est Ravel. Tous ces enregistrements ont été transférés un certain nombre de fois sur microsillon, mais malheureusement à partir de pianos mécaniques qui n'étaient pas toujours bien réglés.

(ii) Enregistrements faits sur disque par trois pianistes qui bénéficièrent tous de conseils détaillés du compositeur : Robert Casadesus (1955, CBS 13062-4 [3]) ; Jacques Février (1972, ADES 7041-4) ; Vlado Perlemuter (1961, VOX VBX 410 1-3 [4] ; 1977, NIMBUS 2101-3, réédition en CD NI 5005, 5011). Marcelle Meyer, qui connaissait Ravel (ils donnèrent ensemble l'exécution à deux pianos de *La Valse* qui ne réussit pas à impressionner Diaghilev), n'étudia jamais sa musique pour piano avec lui, comme sa fille, Marie Bertin, a bien voulu me le confirmer. Je n'ai donc pas tenu compte des enregistrements Ravel de Marcelle Meyer réédités chez EMI dans la collection Référence. Mais je me suis bien entendu référé à l'enregistrement de *Ma mère l'Oye* signé par Casadesus avec son épouse Gaby (1951, Sony Classical MH2K 63316) (**CasrgR**).

(d) Souvenirs de conseils donnés par Ravel sur l'interprétation de sa musique pour piano et rapportés par :

(i) Vlado Perlemuter dans ses entretiens avec Hélène Jourdan-

Morhange, publiés sous le titre *Ravel d'après Ravel* (Lausanne, 1953) ;

(ii) Vlado Perlemuter dans des entretiens avec moi-même ;

(iii) Henriette Faure dans *Mon maître Maurice Ravel* (Paris, 1978) (**FauS**). Ravel fit travailler Henriette Faure, sœur de l'homme politique Edgar Faure, pour le récital – très probablement le tout premier récital de piano entièrement consacré à Ravel – qu'elle donna au théâtre des Champs-Élysées le 12 janvier 1923 (et non le 18 janvier, comme elle le dit dans son livre), à l'âge de dix-huit ans. Sa fille, Mme Mayette Constantin, m'a aimablement informé qu'à une époque elle avait en sa possession les notes originales de sa mère, directement tirées de l'enseignement de Ravel, mais qu'elle les prêta à un chercheur qui ne les lui rendit jamais. Les références d'autres souvenirs sont données dans le texte.

Les sources secondaires sont prises en compte lorsqu'elles jettent une lumière nouvelle sur un texte établi, ou lorsque des problèmes de texte ne sont pas pleinement élucidés par les sources primaires.

Remerciements

J'aimerais remercier les personnes suivantes pour leur aide : Gaby Casadesus, pour les renseignements sur son mari Robert ; Michel Noiray, qui m'a parlé de l'autographe de la *Sonatine* et m'a aidé à en obtenir une copie ; James Segesta, bibliothécaire de California State College, Bakersfield, qui m'a envoyé des copies des partitions corrigées de Lucien Garban ; Jean Touzelet, et ensuite Denis Hall et Rex Lawson, qui m'ont permis d'entendre les rouleaux de piano Duo-Art de Ravel sur une machine en parfait état ; et J. Rigbie Turner, conservateur des manuscrits et livres musicaux de la Pierpont Morgan Library, New York, qui m'a fait parvenir des copies des autographes de *Jeux d'eau*, et de « Noctuelles » et « Oiseaux tristes » de *Miroirs*. Ma reconnaissance va également à deux interprètes : à Roy Howat, qui m'a donné des conseils à la fois musicologiques et pratiques ; à Vlado Perlemuter, qui m'a parlé de ses leçons avec Ravel et m'a permis d'étudier ses partitions. Enfin, ma gratitude va au personnel du département de la musique de la Bibliothèque nationale de France, ainsi qu'à Margaret Cobb, Gwendolyn Mok, Jean-Michel Nectoux, Arbie Orenstein et Stephen Roe pour leurs nombreuses gentillesses, tout spécialement à Graham Hayter de Peters Edition Ltd., Londres, qui a été le pilier de cette entreprise Ravel depuis le début, et dont l'œil perçant et les compétences musicales ont fait de lui (comme le disait Debussy d'André Caplet) « le cimetière des erreurs ».

Roger Nichols
1991

Table des abréviations des sources

A : autographe
E : première édition
CE : exemplaire corrigé de la première édition de Ravel
PerCe : exemplaire imprimé de Perlemuter avec les additions et corrections de Ravel
GarCE : exemplaires imprimés avec les additions et corrections de Garban
GarT : transcriptions pour piano à quatre mains de Garban
RO : transcriptions orchestrales de Ravel
RR : enregistrements de Ravel sur rouleau de piano
CasR : enregistrements de Casadesus
FévR : enregistrements de Février
PerRI et **PerRII** : enregistrements de Perlemuter[5]
PerS(HJM) : souvenirs de Perlemuter dans *Ravel d'après Ravel*, entretiens avec Hélène Jourdan-Morhange
PerS(conv) : souvenirs de Perlemuter, entretiens avec moi-même
FauS : souvenirs d'Henriette Faure, dans *Mon maître Maurice Ravel*

[1] À l'origine Vma. 2967, maintenant recoté Rés. Vma. 493.

[2] Vma. 3157(7) et Fol. Vm12. 2701(2)A respectivement.

[3] Réédition SONY MH2K 63316.

[4] Réédition VOX CDX2 5507

[5] La mention **PerR** sans chiffre indique que les deux enregistrements de Perlemuter coïncident sur le point en question.

LE TOMBEAU DE COUPERIN

Préface

Dans une lettre écrite à son ami Roland-Manuel le 1er octobre 1914, Ravel lui confie qu'il « commence 2 séries de morceaux de piano : 1° une suite française – non ce n'est pas ce que vous croyez : *La Marseillaise* n'y figurera point, et il y aura une forlane, une gigue ; pas de tango, cependant – 2° une *Nuit romantique*, avec spleen, chasse infernale, nonne maudite, etc.[1] ». L'allusion au tango renvoie à l'interdiction de cette danse que venait de décréter l'archevêque de Paris, sous prétexte qu'elle était lascive et offensait les bonnes mœurs (voir également ci-dessous). Peut-être Ravel était-il plus sérieux s'agissant de la gigue et de la *Nuit romantique*, mais en l'occurrence la forlane fut la seule pièce à survivre.

Ravel avait commencé la suite en juillet ce cette année, mais nous ne savons pas précisément ce qu'il avait écrit avant de s'engager comme chauffeur de camion dans l'armée en mars 1915. Marcel Marnat dit que le titre *Le Tombeau de Couperin* fut choisi avant la guerre, et qu'il ne faut donc pas y voir la moindre nuance funèbre [2]. Et le compositeur lui-même disait : « L'hommage s'adresse moins en réalité au seul Couperin lui-même qu'à la musique française du XVIIIe siècle[3]. » Mais la dédicace des six pièces à des amis tués au combat et l'urne funéraire qu'il conçut lui-même pour la première édition montrent clairement que, lorsqu'il reprit l'œuvre au moment de sa libération provisoire de l'armée en juin 1917, elle avait acquis de fortes connotations commémoratives. On peut même y associer sa mère, dont la mort en janvier 1917 le laissa affligé – beaucoup de ses amis pensaient qu'il ne s'en remit jamais vraiment –, ainsi que toute la civilisation d'Europe occidentale, qui, selon lui, avait atteint son apogée en ce XVIIIe siècle qu'il aimait tant et avait maintenant disparue à jamais.

Le 7 juillet 1917, Ravel écrivit à son éditeur Jacques Durand : « Le *Tombeau de Couperin* s'élève. Le "Menuet" et le "Rigaudon" sont achevés. Le reste se dessine [4]. » On peut en déduire que les esquisses qui subsistent pour la « Musette » du « Menuet » et pour le « Prélude » et la « Forlane » [5] datent de cette époque. Ensuite, l'on ne sait rien des progrès de la suite avant que Marguerite Long n'en donne la création à la Salle Gaveau le 11 avril 1919, même si une rumeur disait que Ravel ne voulait pas que cette création ait lieu avant que la guerre ne soit finie. L'œuvre remporta un vif succès et dut être intégralement bissée [6]. Marnat souligne à juste titre l'influence de Rameau et de Scarlatti sur l'écriture pianistique (les deux compositeurs étaient peut-être plus appréciés en France alors qu'aujourd'hui) et cite avec approbation le jugement d'Antoine Goléa : l'œuvre représente « la synthèse courageuse et lucide [...] de presque cent cinquante ans de musique, de *Bastien et Bastienne* [de Mozart] à *Iberia* [d'Albeniz] [7] ».

D'après Marguerite Long, la principale exigence de Ravel dans le « Prélude » était qu'on puisse entendre toutes les notes [8]. C'était sans nul doute vrai pour les notes de taille normale, mais pour les ornements, aussi bien ici qu'ailleurs dans l'œuvre, Ravel tenait non seulement à ce qu'ils soient joués sur le temps, mais que l'accent le plus fort tombe sur la première note de l'ornement avec un diminuendo, et même un brouillage des notes qui suivent. Il voulait aussi un peu d'air (des « respirations ») entre les phrases [9].

Pour la « Fugue », il demandait qu'on utilise seulement les doigts, sans mouvement du poignet [10] ; et les doigtés très détaillés de son propre exemplaire, reproduits dans la présente édition, laissent à penser qu'il employait très peu ou pas du tout de pédale.

Comme nous le disions plus haut, la « Forlane » semble avoir été le premier mouvement que Ravel ait décidé de composer. Dans une lettre non datée, mais qui remonte certainement à l'été de 1914, il écrivit du pays Basque à son ami Cipa Godebski :

> « Je turbine à l'intention du pape. Vous savez que cet auguste personnage [...] vient de lancer une nouvelle danse, la forlane. J'en transcris une de Couperin. Je vais m'occuper à la faire danser au Vatican par Mistinguett et Colette Willy en travesti. Ne vous étonnez pas de ce retour à la religion. C'est l'atmosphère natale qui veut ça [11]. »

La forlane, à l'origine une danse de gondoliers, était la seule danse qu'il était permis d'exécuter en présence du pape, en raison de son caractère solennel, non érotique. La société parisienne raffinée essaya de la substituer au dangereux tango quand celui-ci fut interdit, mais sans succès [12].

La forlane transcrite par Ravel est le dernier des sept mouvements du quatrième *Concert royal* de François Couperin [13]. Ravel garda la structure de Couperin, avec des rondeaux séparés par trois couplets (ABACADA), encore que le dernier retour du rondeau, limité aux six dernières mesures et demie, ne soit plus qu'un écho de son énoncé initial ; et, alors que la « Forlane » de Couperin est en *mi* majeur avec le troisième couplet en mineur, Ravel inverse les modes et prolonge ce dernier couplet avec certaines des harmonies les plus extraordinaires qu'il ait jamais écrites (mes. 140-156). La plupart de ces mesures comportent neuf ou dix notes de la gamme chromatique, et les mesures 149 et 150 contiennent chacune les douze. Il n'est pas vraiment surprenant que, lorsque Marguerite Long joua ce passage au chef d'orchestre Camille Chevillard (né en 1859), celui-ci se soit bouché les oreilles [14].

Le « Rigaudon » et le « Menuet » sont les deux mouvements de la suite que Ravel était heureux de jouer en public, notamment lors de sa tournée américaine en 1928. Dans le premier, il demanda de nouveau à Henriette Faure de faire attention aux « respirations » et d'être implacable dans le tempo [15]. Le « Menuet », son quatrième et dernier essai publié dans cette forme après le *Menuet antique* (1895), le mouvement central de la *Sonatine* (1903-1905) et le *Menuet sur le nom d'Haydn* (1909), est sans doute plus complexe qu'il ne paraît à première vue. Comme dans les deux exemples ci-dessus, Ravel juxtapose deux idées à la reprise – ici la « Musette » continue sous le retour du thème initial –, mais, sur un autre plan, on retrouve cette double perspective bien plus tôt dans la pièce, à savoir aux mesures 9-24 où, comme l'a souligné Françoise Gervais, le phrasé de Ravel est en contradiction avec les inflexions naturelles de la mélodie [16]. On note également que les huit premières mesures de l'articulation de main droite sont organisées comme un palindrome – accent/legato/legato/accent –, alors que la main gauche va à l'encontre de cela avec son propre phrasé. (Pour compliquer encore, dans la version orchestrale de Ravel, le phrasé de main gauche est essentiellement le même que celui de l'original pour piano, tandis que le phrasé de la mélodie jouée par le hautbois est assez différent.)

La suite est couronnée par la « Toccata », dont la fin, disait Ravel, était du pur Saint-Saëns [17] – dans sa bouche, un compliment sur l'excellence de sa facture. Le point culminant, selon Henri Gil-Marchex, « nécessite une indépendance des bras dont la technique reste entièrement à acquérir, même après avoir travaillé les *Études transcendantes* de Liszt [18] » ; Perlemuter pense lui aussi que c'est une œuvre virtuose qui doit se jouer en tant que telle [19].

Parmi les dédicataires, Jacques Chariot était un cousin de l'éditeur de Ravel, Jacques Durand, qui travaillait pour la firme familiale – il est également le dédicataire du deuxième mouvement de *En blanc et noir* de Debussy. Jean Cruppi, qui remplaça finalement le sergent Baguerion-Desormeaux comme dédicataire de la « Fugue », était le fils de Mme Jean Cruppi, dont l'influence avait été cruciale lorsqu'il s'était agi de persuader l'Opéra-Comique de monter *L'Heure espagnole* de Ravel en 1911 ; Gabriel Deluc était un vieil ami de Saint-Jean-de-Luz ; Pierre et Pascal Gaudin étaient des frères que Ravel avait connus enfants – ils furent tués par le même obus le jour où ils arrivèrent sur le front ; Jean Dreyfus était le demi-frère de Roland-Manuel ; et Joseph, marquis de Marliave, était un soldat de métier, passionné de musique, qui épousa Marguerite Long en 1906.

Principes d'édition

La majorité des ajouts de l'éditeur sont entre crochets : indications métronomiques, altérations, nuances, articulation, indications « main droite », « main gauche », doigtés (là où il est nécessaire de compléter les indications minimales de Ravel pour les accords), indications *subito*, *simile* et *loco*, et indications de pédale. Les altérations de précaution de **E**, avec ou sans parenthèses, ont été conservées là où elle semblaient utiles. Les doigtés sont tous tirés de l'exemplaire corrigé de la première édition de Ravel (**CE**), à l'exception de l'indication à la mes. 87 du « Prélude » (pouce de main droite), qui est imprimée dans **E**.

Les indications de pédale sont celles de **E**. Les indications de l'éditeur pour enfoncer ou relâcher la pédale « 1 Corde » sont étayées par des notes dans le commentaire critique.

Des phrasés et des liaisons ont été ajoutés ou corrigés pour correspondre aux passages parallèles. Ces changements, avec les liaisons *laisser vibrer* et les points de staccato, ne se distinguent pas dans le texte musical, mais sont répertoriés dans le commentaire critique. Tous les groupements rythmiques irréguliers sont indiqués ici en tant que tels.

Roger Nichols, 1995
Traduction : Dennis Collins

---

[1] M. Ravel : *Lettres, écrits, entretiens*, éd. A. Orenstein (Paris, 1989), 144-145.
[2] M. Marnat : *Maurice Ravel* (Paris, 1986), 437.
[3] « Esquisse autobiographique », *La Revue musicale* (décembre 1938), 22.
[4] *Ravel au miroir de ses lettres*, éd. M. Gerar et R. Chalupt (Paris, 1956), 150.
[5] A. Orenstein : *Ravel, man and musician*, (New York, 1975), 211-212.
[6] Voir note 1, 185.
[7] Voir note 2, 436-437 ; citation d'A. Goléa : *Esthétique de la musique contemporaine* (Paris, 1954).
[8] M. Long : *Au piano avec Ravel* (Paris, 1971).
[9] FauS 88.
[10] *Ibid.*
[11] Voir note 4, 106.
[12] *Ibid.* ; voir aussi note 2, 387.
[13] A. Orenstein : « Some unpublished music and letters by Maurice Ravel », *Music Forum*, iii (1973), 330-331 (planches xiii a et b).
[14] Voir note 8, 96.
[15] Voir note 9.
[16] F. Gervais : « Ambiguïtés ravéliennes », *Maurice Ravel au XXe siècle* (Paris, 1976), 21.
[17] H. Jourdan-Morhange dans **PerS(HJM)** 75.
[18] H. Gil-Marchex : « La technique de piano », *La Revue musicale* (avril 1925), 44.
[19] **PerS(HJM)** 74.

RAVELS KLAVIERMUSIK – NEUE AUSGABE
Editorische Methode und Quellen

Es ist nicht zu leugnen, dass sich ein Gefühl der Aufregung einstellt, wenn man die autographe Handschrift eines musikalischen Meisterwerks in Händen hält, und wenn darüber hinaus das Autograph selbst ein Kunstwerk ist, wie bei Ravel oft der Fall, so wird dieses Gefühl durch ästhetische Eindrücke noch verstärkt. Ebenso wenig ist jedoch zu leugnen, dass Komponisten wie alle Sterblichen fehlbar sind, und dass das Autograph, so schön und aufregend es sein mag, Fehler enthalten kann. Das scheinbar löbliche Unterfangen, auf das zurückzugreifen, was der Komponist ursprünglich schrieb, muss daher mit einer gewissen Portion Allgemeinverstand aufgewogen werden.

Bei Bühnenwerken führen zeitliche, räumliche, finanzielle und persönliche Zwänge ohne Frage oft zu Eingriffen, die der Komponist in keiner Weise begrüßt, die er aber billigen muss, will er die Aufführung nicht gefährden, und die so in die gedruckte Partitur gelangen. Im Falle von Klavierwerken ist der Druck auf den Komponisten bei der Vorbereitung einer Ausgabe jedoch wesentlich geringer (und wird vor allem vom Verleger ausgeübt, der den Verlagsrichtlinien zu entsprechen sucht), so dass Änderungen auf dem Wege von der Handschrift zur Druckausgabe mit größerer Wahrscheinlichkeit dem Willen des Komponisten entsprechen. Natürlich können im Verlauf der Drucklegung Fehler sowohl entstehen als auch korrigiert werden, und wenn allgemeine und musikalische Erwägungen dies vermuten lassen, kann sich das Autograph tatsächlich oft als ein wichtiges Indiz erweisen. In Gesprächen mit zahlreichen Komponisten der Gegenwart aber wurde mir ganz überwiegend versichert, dass sie vielmehr verärgert wären, würden zukünftige Herausgeber ihre sorgsam erarbeiteten gedruckten Partituren übergehen und auf der Suche nach einer angeblich korrekten Lesart automatisch auf ihre originalen Manuskripte zurückgreifen.

Im Falle von Ravels Klaviermusik ist ein solch kritischer Umgang mit handschriftlichen Zeugnissen mehr denn je gerechtfertigt, findet sich doch in der Musikabteilung der Bibliothèque Nationale de France eine gebundene Sammlung von Ravels eigenen Exemplaren fast aller gedruckten Erstausgaben seiner Solowerke für Klavier samt autographer Korrekturen.[1] Dem Inhalt nach zu urteilen wurde der Band wohl zwischen 1911 und 1913 zusammengestellt. Bei den fehlenden Werken handelt es sich um die *Sérénade grotesque*, *Sites auriculaires*, *Ma mère l'oye*, *Prélude*, *A la manière de…*, *Le tombeau de Couperin* und *Frontispice*. Gedruckte Ausgaben von *Ma mère l'oye* und *A la manière de…* mit autographen Korrekturen finden sich an anderem Ort in derselben Bibliothek[2], während Ravels eigenes Druckexemplar von *Le tombeau de Couperin* mit eigenhändigen Fingersätzen und einer einzigen autographen Korrektur im Musée Ravel in Montfort l'Amaury ausgestellt ist. Bei der *Sérénade grotesque* und *Sites auriculaires* können die Autographen als vorrangige Quellen betrachtet werden, da diese Werke nicht zu Lebzeiten des Komponisten veröffentlicht wurden. Die Eigenschrift von *Frontispice* ist ebenfalls von Bedeutung, da Ravels eigene gedruckte Ausgabe verschollen ist. Für *Prélude* liegt leider weder das Autograph noch das Druckexemplar des Komponisten vor.

Nach aktuellem Kenntnisstand existieren keine Korrekturabzüge der Erstausgaben von Ravels Klavierwerken außer einem Satz Erstkorrekturfahnen von *Le tombeau de Couperin* im Archiv von Durand, die von einem Durand-Lektor berichtigt und mit einer Bitte um Zweitkorrekturabzüge versehen wurden. (Herzlich möchte ich Roy Howat danken, der mir eine Kopie dieses Materials zur Verfügung stellte.) Dieser Satz enthält keine autographen Eintragungen. Sämtliche Korrekturanweisungen wurden in der Erstausgabe berücksichtigt, mit Ausnahme der Gestaltung einiger Mehrfach-Vorschläge in „Prélude" und „Forlane" von *Le tombeau de Couperin*, bezüglich derer augenscheinlich Ravel seine Meinung änderte.

Hauptquellen

Wo Ravels eigenes korrigiertes Exemplar verfügbar war, wurde dieses als Hauptquelle zugrunde gelegt; Abweichungen zwischen dieser korrigierten Ausgabe (**CE**), der gedruckten Erstausgabe (**E**) und dem Autograph (**A**) sind entsprechend vermerkt. Eine weitere Hauptquelle ist die Sammlung von Druckausgaben aus dem Besitz von Vlado Perlemuter, der im Jahre 1927 fast alle Klavierwerke Ravels mit dem Komponisten einstudierte (**PerCE**). Diese Exemplare enthalten einige wertvolle Ergänzungen und Korrekturen von Ravels eigener Hand, vor allem zu *Gaspard de la nuit*. Darüber hinaus finden sich Ergänzungen und Korrekturen von Perlemuters Hand, die er auf Anweisung Ravels vornahm; diese wurden nicht als primäres Quellenmaterial behandelt. Die Exemplare von Robert Casadesus befinden sich nunmehr im Besitz seiner Witwe, doch teilte mir Mme Casadesus freundlicherweise mit, dass darin keine autographen Eintragungen des Komponisten enthalten sind. Ebenso versicherte mir Jacques Févriers Nichte und Schülerin Mme Aboulker-Rosenfeld, dass die Ausgaben ihres Onkels abgesehen von seinen eigenen Fingersätzen keine Eintragungen aufweisen.

Nebenquellen

Die Nebenquellen gliedern sich in vier Gruppen:

(a) Druckexemplare mit Korrekturen von Lucien Garban (**GarCE**). Garban arbeitete für den Verlag Durand und war ein enger Freund des Komponisten. Der genaue Rang dieser Korrekturen ist nicht festzustellen, doch angesichts der Verbindung der beiden ist es denkbar, dass zumindest ein Teil der Änderungen auf Ravel zurückgeht. Diese Exemplare befinden sich nun in der der Bibliothek des Bakersfield College in Kalifornien. Garban bearbeitete darüber hinaus die *Valses nobles et sentimentales* sowie *Le tombeau de Couperin* für Klavier zu vier Händen (**GarT**). Diese Transkriptionen werden von Durand verlegt.

(b) Ravels eigene Orchestrierungen etlicher seiner Klavierstücke (**RO**). In chronologischer Reihenfolge der Erstkomposition (Jahr der Orchestrierung in Klammern) umfassen diese: das *Menuet antique* (1929), die „Habanera" aus *Sites auriculaires* (1908), *Pavane pour une Infante défunte* (1910), „Une barque sur l'océan" und „Alborada del gracioso" aus den *Miroirs* (1906 und 1923), *Ma mère l'oye* (1911), *Valses nobles et sentimentales* (1912) sowie „Prélude", „Forlane", „Menuet" und „Rigaudon" aus *Le tombeau de Couperin* (1919).

(c) Einspielungen

(I) Klavierrollen (**RR**), die Ravel 1913 für Welte-Mignon einspielte (*Sonatine*, 1. und 2. Satz, C2887; *Valses nobles et sentimentales*, C2888) und 1922 für Duo-Art (*Pavane pur une Infante défunte*, 084; „Oiseaux tristes" aus den *Miroirs*, 082). Es ist behauptet worden, dass Ravel bei dieser zweiten Gelegenheit auch „Le gibet" aus *Gaspard de la nuit* und die „Toccata" aus *Le tombeau de Couperin* aufgenommen habe, doch wurden diese vielmehr von Robert Casadesus aufgezeichnet. Es bleibt fraglich, welcher der beiden 1929 für Duo-Art „La vallée des cloches" aus *Miroirs* einspielte (72750), obwohl der Herausgeber sich nahezu sicher ist, dass es Ravel war. All diese Einspielungen sind verschiedentlich auf LP übertragen worden, doch leider war die Klavierrollen-Wiedergabe dabei nicht immer optimal eingestellt.

(II) Schallplattenaufnahmen dreier Pianisten, die sämtlich in den Genuss genauer Anweisungen vom Komponisten kamen: Robert Casadesus (1955, CBS 13062–4[3]); Jacques Février (1972, ADES 7041–4); Vlado Perlemuter (1961, VOX VBX 410 1–3[4]; 1977, NIMBUS 2101–3, später erschienen als CD NI 5005, 5011) (**CasR, FévR, PerRI und PerRII**). Marcelle Meyer war zwar mit Ravel bekannt (sie gaben zusammen jene Privataufführung von *La Valse* auf zwei Klavieren, welche Diaghilev bekanntermaßen unbeeindruckt ließ), doch studierte sie seine Klavierwerke nie mit ihm ein, wie mir ihre Tochter Marie Bertin freundlicherweise mitteilte. Ich habe daher Mme Meyers Ravel-Aufnahmen, die von EMI beim Label Référence neu veröffentlicht wurden, außer Acht gelassen.

(d) Erinnerungen an Ravel als Vermittler seiner Klaviermusik

(I) von Vlado Perlemuter in seinen Interviews mit Hélène Jourdan-Morhange, veröffentlicht als *Ravel d'après Ravel* (Lausanne 1953) sowie in der englischen Übersetzung von F. Tanner als *Ravel according to Ravel* (New York/London 1988; 2/1991) (**PerS(HJM)**)

(II) von Vlado Perlemuter im Gespräch mit dem Herausgeber der vorliegenden Ausgabe (**PerS(conv)**).

(III) von Henriette Faure in *Mon maître Maurice Ravel* (Paris 1978) (**FauS**). Mlle Faure, die Schwester des Politikers Edgar Faure, nahm anlässlich ihres Recitals seiner Musik im Théâtre des Champs-Elysées am 12. Januar 1923 (nicht am 18. Januar, wie in ihrem Buch behauptet) – wahrscheinlich das erste Recital überhaupt, das ausschließlich Ravel gewidmet war – im Alter von 18 Jahren Unterricht beim Komponisten. Auf andere Erinnerungen wird an Ort und Stelle verwiesen.

Die Nebenquellen sind immer dort einbezogen, wo sie zusätzliche Erkenntnisse über die etablierte Lesart vermitteln oder wo Probleme des Notentextes nicht anhand der Hauptquellen gelöst werden konnten.

Danksagungen

Ich danke den folgenden Personen für ihre freundliche Unterstützung: Gaby Casadesus für Informationen über ihren Gatten Robert; Dr. Michel Noiray, der mich auf das Autograph der *Sonatine* aufmerksam machte und mir bei der Beschaffung einer Kopie behilflich war; James Segesta, Bibliothekar beim Leserdienst des California State College in Bakersfield, der mir Kopien der korrigierten Exemplare von Lucien Garban zusandte; Jean Touzelet, der es mir ermöglichte, Ravels Duo-Art-Klavierrollen auf einem einwandfrei funktionierenden Gerät anzuhören; und Dr. J. Rigbie Turner, Leiter der Abteilung für Musikhandschriften und -bücher in der Piepont Morgan Library in New York, für die Zusendung von Kopien der Autographen von *Jeux d'Eau* sowie von „Noctuelles" und „Oiseaux tristes" aus *Miroirs*. Darüber hinaus bin ich zwei ausübenden Musikern zu Dank verpflichtet: Roy Howat für seine Ratschläge, die stets Wissenschaft und Praxis zu vereinbaren wussten; und Vlado Perlemuter, der mit mir über seinen Unterricht bei Ravel sprach und es mir gestattete, seine Notenausgaben durchzusehen. Schließlich danke ich den Mitarbeitern der Musikabteilung der Bibliothèque Nationale de France sowie Margaret Cobb, Gwendolyn Mok, Jean-Michel Nectoux, Dr. Arbie Orenstein und Dr. Stephen Roe für zahlreiche freundliche Hilfeleistungen, und ganz besonders Graham Hayter von Peters Edition Ltd., London, der von Anfang an die tragende Figur dieses Ravel-Vorhabens war und dessen geübtes Auge und Musikverstand ihn (wie Debussy einmal von André Caplet sagte) zum „Friedhof der Druckfehler" machten.

Roger Nichols, 1991

Verzeichnis der Quellensiglen

A: Autograph
E: Erstausgabe
CE: Ravels korrigiertes Exemplar der Erstausgabe
PerCE: Perlemuters Druckexemplar mit Zusätzen und Korrekturen von Ravel
GarCE: Druckexemplare mit Zusätzen und Korrekturen von Garban
GarT: Garbans Bearbeitungen für Klavier zu vier Händen
RO: Ravels Orchesterbearbeitungen
RR: Ravels Einspielungen auf Klavierrolle
CasR: Einspielungen von Casadesus
FévR: Einspielungen von Février
PerRI und **PerRII**: Einspielungen von Perlemuter[5]
PerS(HJM): Erinnerungen von Perlemuter in *Ravel d'après Ravel*, im Gespräch mit Hélène Jourdan-Morhange[6]
PerS(conv): Erinnerungen von Perlemuter im Gespräch mit dem Herausgeber
FauS: Erinnerungen von Faure in *Mon maître Maurice Ravel*

---

[1] Ursprünglich Vma. 2967, nunmehr unter der Signatur Rés. Vma. 493.
[2] Vma. 3157(7) bzw. Fol. Vm12. 2701(2)A
[3] Später erschienen als SONY MH2K 63316.
[4] Später erschienen als VOX CDX2 5507.
[5] Die Bezeichnung **PerR** ohne Nummer bedeutet, dass die zwei Aufnahmen Perlemuters in Bezug auf den fraglichen Punkt übereinstimmen.
[6] Doppelte Seitenangaben beziehen sich jeweils auf die französische und englische Ausgabe.

LE TOMBEAU DE COUPERIN
Vorwort

In einem Brief an seinen Freund Roland-Manuel vom 1. Oktober 1914 teilte Ravel ihm mit, er habe „2 Zyklen von Klavierstücken begonnen: 1. eine französische Suite – nein, nicht so wie Du denkst: die *Marseillaise* wird nicht darin vorkommen, dafür werden eine Forlane und eine Gigue dabei sein; allerdings kein Tango; 2. eine *Romantische Nacht* mit Schwermut, infernalischer Jagd, verfluchter Nonne usw."[1]. Die Tango-Anspielung bezog sich auf das kurz vorher vom Erzbischof von Paris verhängte Verbot dieses Tanzes, der lüstern sei und die öffentliche Moral untergrabe (siehe auch weiter unten). Es ist gut möglich, dass Ravel es mit der Gigue und der *Romantischen Nacht* ernster meinte, doch blieb am Ende von seiner Liste nur die Forlane übrig.

Ravel hatte die Suite im Juli desselben Jahres begonnen, doch sind uns nur vereinzelte Zeugnisse darüber erhalten, wie weit die Komposition gediehen war, als er sich im März 1915 als Lastwagenfahrer zum Militärdienst meldete. Marcel Marnat zufolge stand der Titel *Le tombeau de Couperin* schon vor dem Krieg fest, daher sei nicht davon auszugehen, dass seine begräbnisartigen Anklänge von Anfang an beabsichtigt gewesen seien[2]; und auch der Komponist selber erklärte, dass „die Ehrbezeugung nicht so sehr der Gestalt Couperins im Besonderen als vielmehr der gesamten französischen Musik des 18. Jahrhunderts"[3] gelte. Sowohl Ravels letztendliche Entscheidung, die sechs Stücke gefallenen Freunden zu widmen, als auch die Totenurne, die er für die Titelseite der Erstausgabe entwarf, lassen aber keinen Zweifel, dass die Suite für ihn in starkem Maße den Charakter eines Gedenkstücks angenommen hatte, als er die Arbeit nach seiner vorläufigen Entlassung aus dem Militärdienst im Juni 1917 wieder aufnahm. Zur Reihe jener, deren Verlust er beklagte, ließe sich außerdem seine Mutter zählen, über deren Tod im Januar 1917 er untröstlich war und nach Ansicht vieler Freunde nie hinwegkam, sowie die gesamte westeuropäische Zivilisation, die seiner Meinung nach ihren Höhepunkt im geliebten 18. Jahrhundert erreicht hatte und nun auf immer erloschen war.

Am 7. Juli 1917 schrieb Ravel an seinen Verleger Jacques Durand: „Mit dem *Tombeau de Couperin* komme ich voran. Das Menuett und der Rigaudon sind fertig. Der Rest nimmt Gestalt an."[4] Daraus lässt sich folgern, dass die erhaltenen Skizzen zur „Musette" des „Menuet" sowie zum „Prélude" und zur „Forlane"[5] aus dieser Zeit stammen. Danach ist nichts über den weiteren Fortschritt der Suite bekannt, bis sie am 11. April 1919 in der Salle Gaveau von Marguerite Long uraufgeführt wurde, obwohl es Gerüchten zufolge Ravels Wunsch war, dass die Premiere erst nach Ende des Krieges stattfinde. Das Werk fand großen Anklang und musste als Zugabe komplett wiederholt werden[6]. Marnat weist mit Recht auf den Einfluss von Rameau und Scarlatti auf das tasteninstrumentale Idiom hin (beide Komponisten waren damals in Frankreich wohl populärer als heutzutage) und zitiert zustimmend

Antoine Goléas Urteil, dass das Werk „die mutige, scharfsichtige Synthese von fast hundertfünfzig Jahren Musik, von [Mozarts] *Bastien et Bastienne* bis [Albéniz'] *Iberia*"[7] darstelle.

Laut Marguerite Long verlangte Ravel vor allem, dass im „Prélude" jede Note zu hören sein sollte[8]. Dies galt zweifellos für die Noten im Normaldruck, doch hinsichtlich der Verzierungen, sowohl hier wie auch im Rest des Werks, bestand Ravel darauf, dass sie nicht nur auf dem Schlag zu spielen seien, sondern darüber hinaus die Anfangsnote des Ornaments am stärksten zu betonen sei, gefolgt von einem Diminuendo, sogar einer gewissen Unschärfe der Folgenoten. Er wünschte außerdem kurze Atempausen („*respirations*") zwischen den Phrasen[9].

Bei der „Fugue" wollte er nur die Finger benutzt wissen, ohne Bewegung des Handgelenks[10], und der überaus detaillierte Fingersatz in seinem eigenen Exemplar, in der vorliegenden Ausgabe wiedergegeben, deutet darauf hin, dass er das Pedal – wenn überhaupt – nur wenig gebrauchte.

Wie oben erwähnt, war die „Forlane" offenbar der erste Satz, auf den Ravel sich festlegte. In einem undatierten, aber mit Sicherheit vom Sommer 1914 stammenden Brief schrieb er aus dem Baskenland an seinen Freund Cipa Godebski:

> „Ich rackere mich gerade im Name des Papstes ab. Wie Du weißt, hat diese illustre Persönlichkeit vor kurzem einen neuen Tanz eingeführt, die Forlane. Ich bin dabei, eine von Couperin zu übertragen. Ich werde dafür sorgen, dass sie im Vatikan von Mistinguet und Colette sie in Männerkleidung vorgetanzt wird. Wundere Dich nicht über diese Rückwendung zur Religion. Das macht der Aufenthalt in meiner heimatlichen Umgebung."[11]

Die Forlane, ursprünglich ein Tanz der Gondoliere, war der einzige Tanz, der dank seinem förmlichen und sittsamen Charakter in Anwesenheit des Pontifex aufgeführt werden durfte. Die vornehme Pariser Gesellschaft versuchte ihn als Ersatz für den lasterhaften Tango zu etablieren, nachdem dieser verboten worden war, jedoch ohne Erfolg[12].

Die von Ravel übertragene Forlane ist der letzte der sieben Sätze von François Couperins viertem *Concert royal*[13]. Ravel übernahm Couperins *Rondeaux*-Struktur mit drei eingeschobenen *Couplets* (ABACADA), wobei die letzte Rückkehr des *Rondeau* sechseinhalb Takte vor Schluss nur noch ein Schatten seiner ursprünglichen Gestalt ist; und während Couperins „Forlane" in E-Dur steht, mit dem dritten *Couplet* in Moll, kehrt Ravel die Tongeschlechter um und erweitert dieses letzte *Couplet* um einige sogar für seine Musik außergewöhnliche Harmonien (Takt 140–156). Die meisten dieser Takte enthalten neun oder zehn Töne der chromatischen Tonleiter, die Takte 149 und 150 sogar jeweils alle zwölf. Es verwundert daher nicht sonderlich, dass der Dirigent Camille Chevillard (geboren 1859) sich die Ohren zuhielt, als Marguerite Long ihm diese Passage vorspielte[14].

Der „Rigaudon" und das „Menuet" waren die zwei Sätze der Suite, die Ravel bereit war öffentlich aufzuführen, vor allem auf seiner Konzertreise durch Amerika 1928. In ersterem bat er Henriette Faure, wiederum auf die „*respirations*" zu achten und das Tempo rigoros einzuhalten[15]. Das „Menuett", seine vierte und letzte veröffentlichte Auseinandersetzung mit dieser Form nach dem *Menuet antique* (1895), dem Mittelsatz der *Sonatine* (1903–1905) und dem *Menuet sur le nom d'Haydn* (1909), ist vielleicht komplexer als es zunächst scheint. Wie in den ersten beiden der genannten Beispiele kombiniert Ravel auch hier in der Reprise zwei kontrastierende musikalische Gedanken – die „Musette" läuft weiter, während darüber das Eingangsthema wieder einsetzt –, doch diese Doppelbödigkeit findet sich auf anderer Ebene bereits sehr viel früher im Stück, nämlich in den Takten 9–24, wo Ravels Phrasierung – wie Françoise Gervais bemerkt – dem natürlichen Fluss der Melodie zuwider läuft[16]. Es lässt sich zudem festhalten, dass die Artikulation der rechten Hand in den ersten acht Takten palindromartig angelegt ist – betont/legato/legato/betont –, während die linke Hand dieses Schema mit ihrer eigenen Phrasierung durchbricht. (Und um es noch komplizierter zu machen, übernimmt Ravel diese Phrasierung der linken Hand für seine Orchesterbearbeitung praktisch unverändert aus der Klaviervorlage, phrasiert die Melodielinie der Oboe jedoch ganz anders.)

Den krönenden Abschluss der Suite bildet die „Toccata", deren Ende nach Ravels eigener Aussage reinster Saint-Saëns ist[17] – aus seinem Munde ein Lob ihrer ausgezeichneten handwerklichen Ausführung. An ihrem Höhepunkt verlangt sie mit den Worten von Henri Gil-Marchex „eine Unabhängigkeit der Arme, die man sich speziell erarbeiten muss, selbst nachdem man Liszt's *Transzendentale Etüden* geübt hat"[18], und Perlemuter pflichtet bei, dass sie ein Virtuosenstück sei und als solches gespielt werden müsse[19].

Was die Widmungsträger betrifft, so war Jacques Charlot ein Cousin von Ravels Verleger Jacques Durand und arbeitete für den Familienbetrieb – ihm ist auch der zweite Satz von Debussys *En blanc et noir* zugeeignet; Jean Cruppi, der am Ende die Stelle von Sergeant Baguerion-Desormeaux als Widmungsträger der „Fugue" einnahm, war der Sohn von Mme Jean Cruppi, deren Einfluss im Jahre 1911 ausschlaggebend für die Entscheidung der Opéra-Comique gewesen war, Ravels *L'heure espagnole* auf den Spielplan zu setzen; Gabriel Deluc war ein alter Freund aus Saint-Jean-de-Luz; Pierre und Pascal Gaudin waren Zwillinge, die Ravel aus Kindertagen kannte – sie kamen am Tag ihrer Ankunft an der Front zusammen bei einem Granatenangriff ums Leben; Jean Dreyfus war Roland-Manuels Halbbruder; und Joseph, Marquis de Marliave war ein Berufssoldat mit regem Interesse an Musik und seit 1906 mit Marguerite Long verheiratet.

Editorische Richtlinien

Die Mehrzahl der editorischen Zusätze ist durch eckige Klammern gekennzeichnet: Metronomangaben, Versetzungszeichen, Pausen, dynamische und Artikulations-Bezeichnungen, *main droite*/*main gauche*-Anweisungen, Fingersätze (wo Ergänzungen zu Ravels minimalen Angaben bei Akkorden erforderlich waren), die Hinweise *subito*, *simile* und *loco* sowie Pedalangaben. Warnungsakzidenzien aus **E**, mit oder ohne runde Klammern, wurden beibehalten, wo sie hilfreich erschienen. Die Fingersätze entstammen sämtlich Ravels korrigiertem Exemplar der Erstausgabe (**CE**), mit Ausnahme der Angabe in Takt 87 des „Prélude" (rechter Daumen), die in **E** abgedruckt ist.

Die Pedalangaben folgen **E**. Die Pedalbezeichnungen des Herausgebers bezüglich der Verwendung und Aufhebung von „1 Corde" werden im Kritischen Bericht erläutert.

Phrasierungen und Bindebögen wurden im Einklang mit Parallelstellen hinzugefügt oder berichtigt. Diese Eingriffe sowie zusätzliche *laisser vibrer*-Bindebögen und Stakkatopunkte sind nicht im Notentext gekennzeichnet, aber im Kritischen Bericht aufgeführt. Alle rhythmisch abweichenden Notengruppen sind hier als solche gekennzeichnet.

Roger Nichols, 1995
Übersetzung: Arne Muus

---

[1] M. Ravel: *Lettres, écrits, entretiens*, hrsg. v. A. Orenstein, Paris 1989, 155f. [Engl. Übers. v. A. Orenstein, New York 1990]
[2] M. Marnat: *Maurice Ravel*, Paris 1986, 437
[3] „Esquisse autobiographique", in: *La Revue Musicale* (Dez. 1938), 22
[4] *Ravel au miroir de ses letters*, hrsg. v. M. Gerar / R. Chalupt, Paris 1956, 150
[5] A. Orenstein: *Ravel, man and musician*, New York 1975, 211f. [Dtsch. Übers. v. D. Klose als Maurice Ravel, Leben und Werk, Stuttgart 1978]
[6] Vgl. Anm. 1, 185.
[7] A. Goléa: *Esthétique de la musique contemporaine*, Paris 1954; zit. n. Anm. 2, 436f.
[8] M. Long: *Au piano avec Ravel*, Paris 1971, 94 [Engl. Übers. v. O. Senior-Ellis, London 1973]
[9] FauS 88
[10] *Ebd.*
[11] Vgl. Anm. 4, 106.
[12] *Ebd.*; vgl. auch Anm. 2, 387.
[13] A. Orenstein: „Some unpublished music and letters by Maurice Ravel", in: *Music Forum* 3 (1973), 330f. (Tafeln XIIIa und b)
[14] Vgl. Anm. 8, 96.
[15] Vgl. Anm. 9.
[16] F. Gervais: „Ambiguités raveliennes", in: *Maurice Ravel au XXe siècle*, Paris 1976, 21
[17] H. Jourdan-Morhange, in PerS(HJM) 75/79
[18] H. Gil-Marchex: „La technique de piano", in: *La Revue Musicale* (April 1925), 44
[19] PerS(HJM) 74/78

Le tombeau de Couperin

I: Prélude

à la mémoire du lieutenant Jacques Charlot

Maurice Ravel
(1875-1937)

1) Les petites notes doivent être frappées sur le temps
The grace notes must be played on the beat

II: Fugue
à la mémoire du sous-lieutenant Jean Cruppi

III: Forlane

à la mémoire du lieutenant Gabriel Deluc

1) Les petites notes doivent être frappées sur le temps
   The grace notes must be played on the beat

IV: Rigaudon

à la mémoire de Pierre et Pascal Gaudin

1) Les petites notes doivent être frappées sur le temps
   The grace notes must be played on the beat

V: Menuet
à la mémoire de Jean Dreyfus

1) Les petites notes doivent être frappées sur le temps
   The grace notes must be played on the beat

VI: Toccata

à la mémoire du capitaine Joseph de Marliave

CRITICAL COMMENTARY

Sources: the autograph (18 pp), signed and dated "juillet 1914, juin-novembre 1917", is in the collection of Madame A. Taverne, Monaco. It was not made available for the preparation of this edition. However, part of page 1 (title and elements of bars 1-9) - **A** - appears on the cover of Marguerite Long: *Au piano avec Maurice Ravel* (Paris, 1971)

E - first edition published by Durand (D. & F. 9569), deposited at the Bibliothèque Nationale, Paris, 25 May 1918

For details of all other sources see 'Editorial Method and Sources', p. 3. A table of Source abbreviations appears on p. 4

Prélude

A, E: no metronome marking. Editorial ♩.=92 supported by **RO**

Bars 2, 4, 31, 33, 38, 40, 50, 52, 87, 89. RH beats 1 and 2, if we assume RH ornaments in these bars to be similar, then Ravel's 3-4-2 fingering at start of bar 38 means that, contrary to what has been sometimes claimed, the a' (e' in bars 50, 52, 87, 89) is to be replayed, not tied to the first grace note

Bar 14. **E**: RH beat 2, semiquaver rest. Amended editorially to d' in round brackets

Bar 22. RH beat 1, Ravel's 3-1-2 fingering dispels any doubts regarding articulation of ornament. See note to bars 2, 4 etc.
PerS(conv), FauS 87,90: ...but in all cases, tenuto to be applied to first grace note, synchronised with LH, on the beat; second grace note and main note to be less distinct

Bar 40. **E**: LH beats 1 and 3, F♮s, no *laisser vibrer* ties. Added editorially by analogy with parallel passages

Bar 59. **E**: RH beats 1-2, *laisser vibrer* tie extends from second d♯ to beginning of beat 3. Dotted quaver d♯ inserted editorially at beat 2 (tied to previous note) by analogy with bars 55, 58. Supported by **RO**

Bar 60. As for bar 59, an octave higher
E: RH, treble clef before beat 4. Moved editorially to end of bar 59

Bar 68. **E**: crescendo begins on beat 2. Brought forward editorially to begin on beat 1 as in **RO** and by analogy with bar 63

Bar 77. **E**: LH beats 1 and 2, no slur. Added editorially

Bar 86. **E**: LH beat 3, quaver g, no staccato dot. Added editorially by analogy with parallel passages
E: LH beat 4, quaver rest above B. Augmentation dot added editorially

Bar 90. **E**: RH, *laisser vibrer* tie from g extends to end of beat 2. Shortened editorially by analogy with parallel passages

Bar 91. Editorial *mf* supported by **RO**
Bar 93. Editorial *p* supported by **RO**
Bar 96. Editorial *f* supported by **RO**

Fugue

E: no metronome marking. ♩=84 found in later editions, but provenance unclear; Perlemuter says it came from Marguerite Long. Added editorially

Bar 12. RH beat 3, round brackets to b' added editorially

Bar 14. **E**: redundant diminuendo on final quaver. Deleted editorially. *Subito* added editorially to *pp* in bar 15

Bar 16. **CE**: beat 3, Ravel indicates f'♯ and e' to be taken by LH

Bar 19. **CE**: beats 3 and 4, Ravel indicates g', f''♯ and a' to be taken by LH

Bar 30. **E**: RH beat 1, slur from bar 29 ends incorrectly on d'♯. Repositioned editorially to end on f♯ in LH, beat 1

Bar 34. **E**: lower stave, no slur. Added editorially by analogy with LH of bar 32

Bar 47. **E**: RH beat 3, no augmentation dot to e'. Supplied editorially

Bar 50. **E**: RH beat 4, staccato dot above tied d''. Deleted editorially

Forlane

E: no metronome marking. Editorial ♩.=96 supported by **RO**

Bar 1. **PerS(HJM)** 66/71: "Ravel asked me not to put too much weight on the last quaver [b' of beat 1]; it merely hesitates before the second beat. It's only a touch away from being a grace note." ("Ravel m'avait demandé de ne pas alourdir la croche piquée, elle hésite simplement avant le 2ème temps. De là à la faire comme une petite note, il y a une nuance")

Bars 5-6. **E**: RH slur begins on first b'♯ of bar 6. Amended editorially to begin on d''♯ of bar 5 by analogy with parallel passages

Bar 10. **E**: RH beat 2, no augmentation dot to b''. Supplied editorially

Bar 19. **E**: soft pedal release not indicated. May be held until end of bar 24

Bar 23. **E**: RH beat 1, no augmentation dots to a' and d''. Supplied editorially. Present in **RO** (strings)

Bar 28. **PerS(HJM)** 67/72: "Ravel insisted on all the repeats." ("Ravel tenait à toutes les reprises.") **PerR** repeats bars 9-28; **CasR, FévR** do not

Bars 29-31, 33-35, 46-48, 50-52. **E**: LH slur extends to RH quaver d' in bars 31, 35, 48, 52. Shortened editorially to end on LH crotchet g

Bars 33, 37, 38. **E**: beat 2, redundant *pp*. Deleted editorially

Bar 38, 39. **E**: no crescendo. Present in **RO**

Bar 39. **E**: LH beat 2, tenuto. Deleted editorially

Bar 41. **E**: RH beat 2, dotted crotchet e'♯. **CE**: e'♯ transferred to LH, as printed here

Bars 46-48, 50-52. See note to bars 29-31 etc.

Bar 57. **E**: LH beat 2, no slur. Supplied editorially

Bars 58-59. **E**: RH, separate slurs for bar 58 beat 2 and bar 59 beat 1. Amended to one slur editorially by analogy with bars 4-5, 8-9. Similarly at bars 61-62, 99-100, 103-104

Bars 61-62. See note to bars 58-59

Bars 66. **E**: RH beat 2, no slur. Added editorially by analogy with bar 91

Bars 70, 95. **E**: RH beat 2, tremolo incorrectly notated as dotted quaver. Amended to dotted crotchet editorially

Bar 88. **CE**: RH beat 1, Ravel's fingering $\frac{2}{3}$. Amended editorially

Bars 99-100, 103-104. See note to bars 58-59

Bar 105. **E**: beat 1, C♯/G♯ dyad, dotted crotchet. Amended editorially to dotted minim by analogy with bar 10. **RO**: dotted crotchet tied to quaver on beat 2 in both bars

Bar 114. "1 Corde" suggested editorially by analogy with bar 19

Bar 123. **E**: RH beat 2, slur. Extended editorially to beat 1 of bar 124 by analogy with bars 28-29, 62-63

Bar 135. **E**: LH beat 2, lower part, no augmentation dot to a'. Supplied editorially by analogy with bar 133

Bars 143. **E**: RH beat 2, no slur. Slur to beat 1 of bar 144 extended to begin at f''♯ trill of bar 143. Supported by **RO**

Bars 156, 161. **E**: beat 2, redundant *pp*. Deleted editorially

Bars 161-162. **E:** *laisser vibrer* ties in bar 161 stop short of barline. Extended editorially into bar 162. In **RO** these chords continue for the duration of bar 162 beat 1

Rigaudon

E: no metronome marking. Editorial ♩=120 supported by **RO**

Bars 2, 24, 94, 116. **E:** RH beat 2, quaver joined to semiquavers by quaver beam. Beam deleted editorially in view of articulation and/or changes of dynamic

Bars 9, 13, 16, 20, 101, 105, 108, 112. **E:** LH beat 2. See note to bars 2, 24 etc.

Bar 33. **E:** crescendo continues to bar 34 beat 1. Shortened editorially by analogy with bar 125. Supported by **RO**

Bar 37. **PerS(HJM)** 71/74, 75: Ravel wanted the pianist to imitate the oboe used in **RO**. He also "wanted it without nuance. The tune's continuity is enough in itself." ("Il la voulait sans nuance, la continuité de la mélodie se suffit à elle-même")

Bar 77. Editorial soft pedal release supported by muting of cellos in RO, bars 69-76.

Bar 116. **E:** beat 2, no staccato dots to accented chords. Added editorially by analogy with bar 24

Menuet

E: no metronome marking. ♩=92 found in later editions, but provenance unclear; as with 'Fugue', Perlemuter says it came from Marguerite Long. **RO:** ♩=120. Ideal speed would seem to lie between these extremes: **PerRII** takes 4′53″ (♩=102), **CasR** takes 4′20″ (♩=117). ♩=92-120 added editorially

Bar 1. RH beat 1. By analogy with bar 38 of 'Prélude', it seems logical to play the grace notes as slurred to the crotchet dyad and not to tie the Ds. As elsewhere, tenuto to be applied to first grace note, with following notes less distinct See note to bar 22 of 'Prélude'

Bar 22. **PerS(HJM)** 73/76: "Here many pianists make a diminuendo on the third beat, whereas Ravel asked me to make a continuous crescendo." ("Ici beaucoup de pianistes diminuent sur le 3ème temps, alors que Ravel m'avait demandé un crescendo continu.") Thus in **E**

FauS 90: "In this piece, Ravel's most important observation was to ask me to make a diminuendo through the rising chords on the first page." ("Dans cette pièce l'observation essentielle que me fit Ravel fut de me demander de faire dans la 1ère page les montées d'accords en diminuant.") Thus in **RO**

Bar 25. **E:** RH beat 1, tenuto marking to crotchet. Deleted editorially by analogy with bars 1, 29, 101

Bar 28. **E:** LH, lower part, minim *a* with *laisser vibrer* tie extending to crotchet rest at beat 3. Amended to dotted minim by analogy with bar 100. Supported by **RO** (2nd horn)

Bar 33. **PerS(HJM)** 73/77: "Ravel asked me to play the Musette at the same tempo as the outer sections." ("Ravel m'avait demandé de jouer la Musette dans le même mouvement...")

Bars 41-48. **E:** melody in LH in odd-numbered bars, in RH in even-numbered bars. **PerS(conv):** Ravel preferred melody played in RH throughout. Layout altered editorially

Bar 81. Editorial soft pedal release supported by RO (removal of mutes in 2nd violin, viola, cello)

Bar 95. **E:** RH, lower part, no slur. Added editorially by analogy with bar 23

Bar 104. **E:** redundant *pp* above upper stave. Deleted editorially

Bars 109, 110, 111. Beat 1, editorial tenuto supported by **RO**

Bars 120, 121. **PerS(HJM)** 73/77: "Ah! Ravel wanted this delicate effect [grace notes to beat 1 of bar 121] made quickly and unexpectedly, like a surprise!" ("Ah! Ce petit effet! Ravel, en effet, le voulait rapide et... inattendu, comme une surprise!")

Bars 122, 123. RH beat 1, grace note in this instance tied to minim

Bar 126. **E:** LH trill, no augmentation dot. Supplied editorially

Toccata

E: no metronome marking. ♩=144 found in later editions, but provenance unclear; as with 'Fugue' and 'Menuet', Perlemuter says it came from Marguerite Long. **CasR**, **FévR**, **PerR** range between ♩=130 and ♩=140. ♩=144 added editorially

Bar 119. **E:** LH beat 1, $d''\sharp$ minim. Shortened to crotchet editorially in view of continuation of melody in RH, beat 2

Bar 155. Editorial soft pedal release indicated, but it could be that Ravel wanted soft pedal re-applied at bar 160, or retained from bar 145 through to bar 167 and perhaps beyond

Bars 155-159. **E:** RH, slur ends at crotchet d' of bar 157; new slur begins at e' of same bar. Slurs joined editorially by analogy with bars 168-172

Bar 191. **PerS(HJM)** 75/79: "Here Ravel asked me to begin *piano*, with the soft pedal, to allow room for the crescendo. *Piano*, but intense." ("Ici, Ravel m'avait demandé aussi de commencer piano, avec la sourdine afin de ménager le crescendo, piano, mais intense.") Unfortunately, Ravel did not say where soft pedal should be released

Bars 194, 198. **E:** LH beat 2, quaver rest. Deleted, and editorial crotchet rest supplied

Bar 221. **PerS(HJM)** 75/79: "When the first episode returns with an outburst of regularly alternating chords, Ravel asked me to take it a little slower to give more weight to the accents; then to come back gradually to the opening tempo, but without giving the impression of a gallop!" ("Lorsque le premier épisode est repris dans son éclat d'accords alternés et rythmiques, Ravel m'avait encore demandé de le prendre un peu moins vite pour affirmer les accents, mais en reprenant petit à petit le tempo initial et sans donner une impression de galopade!") But not observed in **PerR**

Bar 244. **E:** LH beat 2, crotchet rest. Deleted editorially

Roger Nichols
1995